COURAGE LEADS
THE WAY

A Guide to Using Your Fears Wisely

COURAGE LEADS
THE WAY

A Guide to Using Your Fears Wisely

By Jonathan Frejuste

Table of Contents

INTRODUCTION

*Jesus became like these people and
died so that he could free them.
They were like slaves all their lives
because of their fear of death.*
Hebrews 2:15, ERV

During an interview, Dr. King said that it doesn't matter how long you live. It matters how well. His very last speech, "I've Been to the Mountaintop," acknowledged that thinking about the future (longevity) has its place. He was a man who believed this message through and through.

Dr. King was receiving death threats for his stances on racism, the Vietnam War, and his rebuke of the exploitation of the poor. In 1968, his days were full of anxiety.

He would give speeches during this time, and actor Harry Belafonte observed that Dr. King had a tic (a slight stutter) when he spoke. One day, Belafonte noticed that the tic went away. He surmised that it had a psychological cause.

He asked Dr. King what he had done to make it go away. Dr King said that he had made his peace with death. Powerful!

This was a man who embraced his mission wholeheartedly. The path wasn't easy, but eventually he settled at this place where he accepted whatever the outcome would be. His legacy continues to shape world leaders for the better.

One conclusion that we can make is that Dr. King was a free man. We can experience that same freedom by understanding what courage is and is not and how to cultivate it.

We all get afraid. Fear is psychologically and physiologically hardwired into human beings to keep us safe. It starts in the brain and then affects how we feel. Ironically, the same thing that can protect you can stand in your way. It can restrict your thinking and keep you from going being boundaries that have been established to hinder ability to walk by faith and not sight or appearance. There's nothing wrong with an emotional reaction to fear. What's important is what happens after.

Brave people are not without fear. They can rise above it and not be paralyzed by it. A lack of courage is often due to misplaced fears which are educated into us through conditioning and proximity. If they are educated into us, they can be educated out of us.

Since fear can't be removed from our nature, we can replace inferior fears with a superior fear. This guide will serve as a curriculum for courage that helps you change the way you think. If you can change the way you think, you can change the way you live.

If you live life taking counsel from fears that don't serve you in creating a life that gives you permission to consider countercultural perspectives and walk in authentic personhood, you'll more than likely live a life full of regrets and minimal impact.

Let this guide provide you with perspectives to consider as you chart your course on the journey of life.

1: COURAGE TO THINK CLEARLY

Clear thinking comes from courage
more than intelligence.

In the mid-nineteenth century, science didn't drive all medical decisions. At the time, it was believed the cause of the deaths was the "miasma theory" caused by poisonous vapors or "bad air."

In 1847, Hungarian physician Ignaz Semmelweis grew frustrated when one out of five new mothers died of childbed fever. Everything was in question for him until he got to the bottom of the problem. He observed that doctors were performing autopsies and then helping to deliver babies without washing their hands.

He asked his fellow doctors and medical students to practice hand hygiene. The death rate from childbed fever significantly dropped. Despite this improvement, hand-washing was met with shocking resistance. Unfortunately, going against the orthodox and conventional best practice wasn't pleasing to everyone. His work irritated his superiors, and his theory was dismissed or attacked in published medical works and rejected by renown physicians. The medical community did not want to change. Dr. Semmelweis made enemies.

Today, his work is seen as obviously groundbreaking and life-saving, but in his own time, he was discredited. He lost his job and spent his days convincing medical professionals to simply wash their hands. Semmelweis didn't live to see the profound impact of his work. Where would the medical profession be without the relentless persistence of Ignaz Semmelweis.

> **Lesson#1:** Just because something is a prevailing practice doesn't mean it's right, true, or meant to be permanent.
>
> *And do not be conformed to this world [any longer with its superficial values and customs], but be transformed and progressively changed [as you mature spiritually] by the renewing of your mind [focusing on godly values and ethical attitudes], so that you may prove [for yourselves] what the will of God is, that which is good and acceptable and perfect [in His plan and purpose for you]. Romans 12:2, AMP*
>
> **Lesson #2:** Develop assertiveness. Ignaz said what other people were afraid to say to the people they were too afraid to say it to.
>
> *They sent their disciples to Him, along with the Herodians, saying, "Teacher, we know that You are sincere and that You teach the way of God truthfully, without concerning Yourself about [what] anyone [thinks or says of Your teachings]; for You are impartial*

and do not seek anyone's favor [and You treat all people alike, regardless of status]. Matthew 22:16, AMP

Lesson #3: Don't be contaminated by manmade customs, practices, and perspectives. You can be corrupted by the same profession that you want to serve. Your ability to stand alone will serve the purpose of doing important work that may save lives.

Pure and unblemished religion [as it is expressed in outward acts] in the sight of our God and Father is this: to visit and look after the fatherless and the widows in their distress, and to keep oneself uncontaminated by the [secular] world. James 1:27, AMP

Lesson#4: Study the issue well enough to have a clear moral position. Preserving neutrality may be wise or it can pass for wisdom when in fact, it is a cover for cowardice and protection of personal gain. "Really, what profit is there for you to gain the whole world and lose yourself in the process?" (Mark 8:36, VOICE)

When you become a drum major for a sea change in an industry or paradigm, expect opposition because evolution leads to a product, idea or method becoming irrelevant or obsolete. Keeping in mind that you are going to eventually die keeps you from the foolish thinking that you have something to lose.

*The wicked flee when no man pursues them, but the **[uncompromisingly] righteous** are bold as a lion. Proverbs 28:1, AMPC*

Don't allow the reaction of others at the inception of your work to determine its legitimacy. Limiting beliefs exist in many industries and sectors of society. If one of the main goals is to make the world better, we need to courage to simply say, "Why is this happening?" and question everything until we find an answer. Then we must be prepared for those who aren't yet ready to change because without planning to change, you're inevitably planning to choose the status quo.

Be afraid of being someone's puppet.

2: COURAGE TO LIVE BY DESIGN, NOT DEFAULT

*Success should be defined based on
the eulogy, not your currency.*

Bryan Stevenson is the author of *Just Mercy, A Story of Justice and Redemption* and the founder of Equal Justice Initiative (www.eji.org), a human rights organization in Montgomery, Alabama. Through his work as a public interest lawyer for the incarcerated, the condemned, and the poor, he has saved dozens of people from the death penalty.

In short, Stevenson's work is a miracle, because he didn't meet a lawyer until he got to law school. By God's grace and his tenacity, he stuck to his ideals and tried to become something he'd never seen.

When he got to Harvard's law school, he was tempted to compromise and settle for a life that he was not meant to live. In school, he didn't hear anything that addressed race, poverty, and inequity—the topics he cared most about. But he refused to become well-adjusted to injustice and pursue the corrupted American Dream of peacocking and posturing.

His dream went further than the American Dream. He had a dream of justice. Believing the dots would connect, he followed his convictions, though it led him off the well-worn path. Part of being courageous is making difficult choices to change your life for the purpose of serving a larger dream, especially when there are no guarantees. It's unreasonable (not guided by good sense based on the ideas of acceptability or fairness of the times) – unreasonable men change the world.

I believe that God gives us lamps, not flashlights, so that we can take the next step even though we can't see the road ahead.

Bryan recognized that it was absurd to have traumatized youth certified to stand trial as adults. From his perspective, if a judge can make you into something that you're not, the judge must have magic ability.

In one of his cases, he was representing a fourteen-year-old black male. He wrote a motion asking the court to treat his fourteen-year-old black client as if he were a white, privileged, seventy-five-year-old corporate executive.

The court was upset. Stevenson began to engage in an argument with the court about the nature of his motion and about race, inequality, and poverty. A black custodian came into the courtroom and sat behind Mr. Stevenson. Although the deputy sheriff rebuked him for being in the courtroom, the black custodian told Stevenson to never lose sight of the prize and to hold on. Bryan Stevenson has won relief for more than 140 people on death row and hundreds of people who were unfairly sentenced or wrongfully convicted.

> *Does this sound like success to you?*

> *Success is not something you chase. It's something you attract based on who you become and what you produce.*

It doesn't matter how well you play the game, if you're playing the wrong game. The life that you live is one that should come from your paradigm, your values, desires, and aspirations. Sadly, most people are living unexamined lives and by the time they realize that they've been climbing a ladder that's leaning against the wrong wall, they have become deeply entrenched in life circumstances that have a steep exit cost. For most people, decisions are not made with common sense. They are made with common agreement. Give yourself to permission to assess and reassess how you design your life.

Reflections on Success

> *Jesus: "If you find the godless*
> *world is hating you, remember it*
> *got its start hating me. If you lived*
> *on the world's terms, the world*
> *would love you as one of its own.*
> *But since I picked you to live on*
> *God's terms and no longer on the*
> *world's terms, the world is going to*
> *hate you."*
>
> **John 15:19, MSG**

Here are few thoughts and reflections on success and failure that have their own unique implications and applications to life. Take note that these definitions may vary and even contradict each other. That's why each of us must develop our own unique definition/understanding of success—because each of us has been uniquely designed. Success is as unique as a fingerprint.

Meditate on who you are and what you want. Develop clarity of intention. Then live it out.

When you uncover the rationale behind your goals, you'll be more motivated. Defining what you believe success is important in determining how to organize your efforts.

Here's a list of different definitions/ideas of success to consider:

1. Success is running the race uniquely designed for me. Nothing is worse than crossing the finish line only to realize that you were in the wrong race.

2. Success is not about where you are in relation to the person next to you. It's about where you are in relation to where you started and what you started with.

3. The greatest fear we should have is in succeeding at things that ultimately don't matter.

4. Success is being respected most by people who know me best.

5. Success is not about starting well but finishing well.

6. Success is not about standing with the greats but sitting with the broken.

While Jesus was having dinner at Levi's house, many tax collectors and sinners were eating with him and his disciples, for there were many who followed him. When the teachers of the law who were Pharisees saw him eating with the sinners and tax collectors, they asked his disciples: "Why does he eat with tax collectors and sinners?" On hearing this, Jesus said to them, "It is not the healthy who need a doctor, but the sick. I have not come to call the righteous, but sinners." (Mark 2:15-17, NIV)

1. Success is doing things that are important, even if they are not impressive.

2. Success is never allowing my ambition to become greater than my gratitude.

I'm glad in God, far happier than you would ever guess—happy that you're again showing such strong concern for me. Not that you ever quit praying and thinking about me. You just had no chance to show it. Actually, I don't have a sense of needing anything personally. I've learned by now to be quite content whatever my circumstances. I'm just as happy with little as with much, with much as with little. I've found the recipe for being happy whether full or hungry, hands full or hands empty. Whatever I have, wherever I am, I can make it through anything in the One who makes me who I am. (Philippians 2:12-13, MSG)

1. Success is refusing to conform to the standards of the people who are "in charge" but submitting to the One who has ultimate authority.

   Am I now trying to win the approval of human beings, or of God? Or am I trying to please people? If I we're still trying to please people, I would not be a servant of Christ. (Galatians 1:10, NIV)

2. People say they want to do things that matter and then measure themselves against things that don't matter.

3. Success is having more ability than visibility to avoid questionable credibility.

4. Your greatest responsibility is to invest in yourself to become clear about what it is you want.

5. Success is making decisions with eternity in mind.
6. Success is contributing more than you criticize.
7. Success is glorifying God by living in a way that makes sense in light of eternity.
8. It makes no difference how fast you are in the 100 meters if the race is 400 meters long.
9. Collective progress is just as important as individual accomplishment.
10. Success is being relevant to your center/core conviction instead of adopting mainstream notions of success.
11. Success is holding onto your principles amid pressure. No amount of applause can dictate success. Otherwise, one can be controlled and compromise on what's right.
12. Success means you replace the words "bigger" and "well-known" with "effective" and "better."

How do these thoughts and reflections resonate with you?

_____

_____

Which one(s) motivate you? In what way(s) do they motivate you?

_____

_____

Do you have your own personal definition(s) of success? It's been suggested that the ideal definition of success includes four elements: contentment, achievement, happiness, and other people.

Be afraid to let someone plan your life.

3: COURAGE TO TAKE RESPONSIBILITY

*Make a careful exploration of who
you are and the work you have
been given, and then sink yourself
into that. Don't be impressed with
yourself. Don't compare yourself
with others. Each of you must take
responsibility for doing the creative
best you can with your own life.*
Galatians 6:5, MSG

There's a story about a legendary designer and master builder who was ready to retire. He'd had an apprentice working under his tutelage for many years. The apprentice was very talented and easily picked up the lessons his mentor taught. Together, they built homes for celebrities, cathedrals, and business buildings. He was ready to become a master builder.

One day, the mentor left him one last project before his retirement. He asked the apprentice to build his retirement home.

In this case, he would not serve as a supervisor to the apprentice, due to his schedule. He left the responsibility of the full development of the project to the apprentice. He gave him full autonomy and a generous budget to use the best materials/supplies/work.

The apprentice commenced the work with excellence. But somewhere along the line, he realized that there was no authority over him, and he started to be lax with his effort. He started to arrive late and leave early, and his precision decreased. He started cutting corners, using inferior products, and not reviewing the work of the other contractors. He put in less effort than he normally did when he had a supervisor.

Because he didn't have a vested interest in the work, he did an overall poor job and subsequently built an inferior home. The mentor came to the home upon completion and as an experienced builder, he could see the inferiority of the work.

When the apprentice handed him the keys to the completed house, the mentor looked down, grabbed the keys, and gave them right back. He said, "Here are the keys to the house you built. It was always meant to be yours."

The apprentice looked at the mentor in surprise and sadness as he slowly and painfully realized that he had lost an opportunity to build the home of his dreams because he didn't care about someone else's reality, and he lacked his own personal standard. The mentor's test was not only to ensure that the mentee knew how to build, but also to determine if the mentee had his own standard of excellence.

If you've ever caught yourself skimping on work, remember that your motivation to do great work should not only be the compensation you receive, but the reputation that you build – not your reputation but the person you represent.

It is important to take responsibility for your cultivating the right attitude, aptitude, and approach to your work and life. Responsibility is something you WEAR.

1. **Willingness to suffer to honor your own personal standard, whether the work will directly serve you or not, because your work is a message.**

    But you must stay calm and be willing to suffer. You must work hard, telling the good news and to do your job well.
    2 Timothy 4:5, CEV

2. **Emotional investment. Supervisors are superfluous. Never work to the level of your paycheck. Be emotionally invested based on self-imposed standards. After some time, the discipline becomes a desire and a habit. What would happen if you were fully present with every opportunity?**

    Use all your strength to do the work that you are doing. One day you will die, and you will go into your

grave. Then you will not have any work, or ideas, or knowledge or wisdom. So do your work well while you are alive.
Ecclesiastes 9:10, EASY

Whatever you do [whatever your task may be], work from the soul [that is, put in your very best effort], as [something done] for the Lord and not for men.
Colossians 3:23, AMP

Whatever you are doing, show that God is great. When you eat anything, or you drink anything, do it all in a way that praises God.
1 Corinthians 10:31, EASY

3. **Attention to Detail. Amateurs do it until it's right. Professionals do it until it can't be done wrong. Aim for mastery in all your work.**

    Do you know a hard-working man? He shall be successful and stand before kings!
    Proverbs 22:29, TLB

    Observe people who are good at their work— skilled workers are always in demand and admired; they don't take a backseat to anyone.
    Proverbs 22:29, MSG

4. **Rigorous Foundation Building - If you want to go high, you must dig deep.** Good ideas won't interrupt you. Taking responsibility requires that you grow your knowledge base because we think to the level of what we're exposed to and cannot rise above the plain of our mental conditioning.

If you have good sense, you will learn all you can, but foolish talk will soon destroy you.
Proverbs 10:14, CEV

"The beginning of wisdom is: Get [skillful and godly] wisdom [it is preeminent]! And with all your acquiring, get understanding [actively seek spiritual discernment, mature comprehension, and logical interpretation].
Proverbs 4:7, AMP

Wisdom is the most important thing. So get wisdom. If it costs everything you have, get understanding.
Proverbs 4:7, NCV

Be afraid of mediocrity and self-sabotage.

4: COURAGE TO BE YOURSELF

In a race everyone runs, but only
one person gets first prize. So run
your race to win.
(1 Corinthians 9:24, TLB)

In a culture of constant comparison and scarcity, our job is to take full control of the individuality we were born with and develop it, without being defeated by the harshness of life.

When you run your own race, you become self-possessed, which means you've taken full ownership and responsibility for your unique, God-given personhood and refuse to be compartmentalized, incarcerated, or institutionalized by the expectations of those who have a limited perspective of you.

If there is a person who exemplifies running their race to the very end, it's one of the most prolific actors of my generation, Chadwick Boseman. He had a great movie career where he played iconic historical figures but was launched into international stardom when he played the role of T'Challa in the Marvel movie Black Panther. He was diagnosed with colon cancer in 2016 and battled until he passed away on August 28, 2020, at the age of forty-three.

Boseman is a man who lived on purpose. In his final speech to his alma mater, Howard University, he discussed the dilemma of the roles he played. At the beginning of his career, he was offered a six-figure job for a soap opera with a major network. During a conversation with the show's executives, who loved his previous episodes, he challenged the stereotypical role of the black character that he was auditioning for. He was fired the next day. His principles closed doors that day. But although he felt building doubt and inner conflict, he stuck to his guns, which might have paved the way for a less-stereotypical role in the future. He thought he might have been blackballed. He was knocked down, and that showed him what fight he was in. He fought back and won!

Here's a list of his works that emphasized social issues that are still relevant today.

- **42 (2013)** – A movie about Jackie Robinson, the first African American to play in Major League Baseball. He was signed to the Brooklyn Dodgers and faced immense racism in the process.
- **Get On Up (2014)** – A movie that describes the life of the legendary artist James Brown and ascent from poverty to superstardom.

- **Marshall (2017)** – A biographical legal drama about the first African American Supreme Court Justice Thurgood Marshall, who was a crusading lawyer and champion of career-defining cases.
- **Black Panther (2018)** – A superhero movie about a leader of an independent African nation who is crowned king after his father's death. He is challenged by his long-lost cousin, who wanted the nation to abandon its isolationist practices and begin a global revolution.
- **21 Bridges (2019)** – A movie about an embattled NYPD detective who uncovers an unexpected conspiracy while on a citywide manhunt of cop killers. The movie captures the nuances of police life.
- **Da 5 Bloods (2020)** – A movie about the grief and emotional life of four African-American veterans who served in Vietnam.
- **Ma Rainey's Black Bottom (2020)** – A movie that depicts a black woman who refused to give her power away and used her gift to help others feel free.

How to nurture your unique sense of self

Each person is certain ways:
- like everyone else
- like some other people
- like no one else

To nurture these ways, there are 3 things you can do to help you along to journey to living in alignment with your unique self.

1. Find your tribe.
2. Learn how to deal with criticism.
3. Be the guardian of your values. Be willing to pay the price for your values.

1. Find your tribe.

Stay away from cliques. Here's how to kn*ow the difference.*

Tribe vs. Clique

Tribes are healthy community environments that nurture each person's unique sense of self and give them permission to act on their purpose. Unhealthy communities are called cliques.

Which community are you part of? Here are five ways you can tell the difference:

1. A **clique** wants everyone to *fit in* instead of *belonging*. Fitting in requires that you check the box of appearance, societal position, titles, skills, possessions, and associations (who you know). A **tribe** doesn't keep track of any of that. You belong and you can come as you are.

2. A **clique** is an institution for people's selfish agendas and there are strings attached. A **tribe** is an incubator for purpose. Each person respects and accepts one another's individuality and provides support as appropriate.

3. A **clique** has a scarcity mentality where the concern is always about lack, which provokes anxiety and unhealthy ambition. A **tribe** has an abundance mentality and believes there are enough resources for everyone.

4. A **clique** is obsessed with unhealthy comparisons to one another and trying to keep up. A **tribe** avoids unhealthy comparisons. People work to be inspired by others instead of jealous. There is a strong encouragement to make decisions with one's unique path and purpose.

5. A **clique** is about exclusivity and invite only. Only the special people can come. A **tribe** is inclusive, because the goal is to help people feel comfortable with their sense of self.

Jonathan Frejuste

2: Learn how to deal with criticism.

Dealing with Criticism

Whenever you step out to do something innovative or different from convention, you will have to deal with critics. Your work may threaten their position or trigger their insecurities, so their criticism will be self-serving. Some criticism will be well-meaning and concerned with the effectiveness of your method or way of operating because others might not recognize what you're trying to do. Your way will be out of context with their point of reference.

You need a framework to determine whose opinion matters as it relates to your approach to your work and how to apply their criticism appropriately and wisely.

Reflection Questions:

1. Are your critics offering any clearly obvious words of correction that you can employ? Your critics can be your coaches, so if their words of correction are actionable, take notes and move forward.
2. Gut check: Are you seeking improvement of your work, or just seeking the approval of the critics? It becomes dangerous to vie for someone's approval because you may lose the freedom spirit needed to stay locked into your work and your way.

a. Note: If you're building your life or creative work in the way someone else does things because you see it working for other people, you're not being authentic.

b. *"There's trouble ahead when you live only for the approval of others, saying what flatters them, doing what indulges them. Popularity contests are not truth contests—look how many scoundrel preachers were approved by your ancestors! Your task is to be true, not popular.* **Luke 6:26, MSG**

    i. If all men speak well of you, that means you're duplicitous and a people pleaser. You can't speak the truth and live out your values without disappointing people.

3. Focus on the purpose, not the criticism. If you magnify the criticism, you'll lose sight of the big picture. See **Simplify Your Purpose: Find Your Lane, There's Less Traffic**

Simplify Your Purpose: Find Your Lane, There's Less Traffic

> *Don't do things that you think will inspire hope. Do the things that bring you hope because those things can inspire hope in others.*

The most fundamental question that people ask children is, "What do you do want to do when you grow up?" This question often asks them to name a particular professional ambition. A better question is, "What do you want your life to be about?" This question speaks to purpose.

In the world of personal development, you often hear phrases like **PSDR**, an acronym for four stages in developing a goal:

Pick your battle.
Start with the end in mind.
Define your success.
ROI (return on investment): What do you want to gain?

These questions speak to specific aims or targets. But before you get too specific, I think you should start the mentorship process with a broader intention: finding your lane.

Each person has a lane in life that they are designed and qualified to travel. If we don't identify that lane, we run the risk of making premature commitments to certain paths. You don't have to be too specific too soon. The journey to your specific destiny is a funnel.

Far too many people have seen their purpose derailed when they went down a path that they were not meant to travel. As a result, their lives are full of poor choices, wasted time, and tons of regret. Use the following exercises to simplify your purpose in this season of your life.

I believe there is power in simplicity.

Exercise: Find Your Path - What do you want to do?

Choose three actions from the list below to find the form of your purpose. Choose actions that resonate with you.

Build — Repair — Learn — Destroy — Teach — Fight — Overcome — Restore — Remove — Correct — Prepare — Change — Remember — Inform — Raise — Alert — Become — Resolve — Determine — Manifest — Promote — Provide — Protect — Encourage — Make — Care — Counsel — Commit — Defend — Ensure — Revive — Break down — Prevent — Instruct — Hold on — Leave behind — Avoid — Invite — Evoke — Invoke — Demystify

If you have any other words you want to include, you can add those words below.

Who do you want to help?
Choose three groups/interest/causes from the list below that you'd like to benefit from your purpose.

Groups/Interests/Causes:

Studies of culture	Business	Animal life	Social justice	Finance
Fitness	Airplanes	Faith	African American History	Music
Space exploration	Law	Nutrition	Child Care	Education

Education	Travel	World history	Great inventors	Family health
Gospel	Mental illness	Community building	World missions	Human development
Community development	Prison Reentry	Literacy	Emotional Health	Cinema

COURAGE LEADS THE WAY

If you have any other groups you want to include, add those words to your choices.

My possible paths include:

Examples: I want to **encourage**   **social justice**.
I want to **protect**   **my family**.
I want to **revive**   **my community**.

I want to _____ (group)

_____

I want to _____ (group)

_____

I want to _____ (group)

_____

Write a purpose statement

We cannot live productively in the absence of purpose. We would never start a business without a mission statement and set of core values. So why do we often skip over identifying a purpose for our own lives?

A clearly defined purpose statement can help us chart our course with confidence and resist our need to please others.

Unfortunately, many focus on obtaining a position or material possessions. These are not necessarily bad goals, but once they obtain the position or the material possessions, they lose enthusiasm.

A **purpose statement** is designed to integrate who you are and what you do. It is the way you start transforming your life from a drifting generality to a meaningful specific. Combine the information you've gotten about your purpose to come up with a statement of your intention. It doesn't have to be perfect, but it must be honest and grounded in reality.

Here's mine:

"To provide quality mentoring tools to underserved, under-resourced, and vulnerable communities in ways that support sustained social change, a restoration of hope, and an avenue to mental and emotional health."

The Bridge330 Mentoring Program

Here's another example:

"To fight against the stigma of mental illness in the black community by inviting people to share their stories in an authentic and safe way."

What's your purpose statement?

_____

_____

_____

The important thing to understand about your purpose is that it's dynamic. Your purpose can and should change, evolve, and grow in complexity or simplicity. I encourage you to use these exercises repeatedly on the road to finding and living in alignment with your purpose.

3: Be the Guardian of Your Values

Remind yourself that you are the guardian of your values. You have to nourish and protect them. Historically, the people we remember most are the ones who paid a heavy price for their values:

Nelson Mandela: One that always stands out is the model shown by Nelson Mandela. Seeing the unfairness and oppressiveness of the apartheid regime of South Africa, Mandela joined the struggle to put an end to it. The South African government did not take long to take note of this bold attorney. He was arrested alongside other political stalwarts. He was tried and sentenced to life in prison where he spent the next 27 years until his release in 1990. He was deprived of his right to be with his family and friends. He lost 27 years of his life. He was in isolation and his human rights were violated. He had every right to be angry. He could have sought revenge but when he got out of prison, he preached reconciliation and forgiveness.

Value: Justice

Dr. Martin Luther King Jr., Martin Luther King, Jr. and his family over the course of his work as a civil rights leader faced many death threats, yet he continued to work. He believed that no matter how deeply someone sank into racial hatred, that person could be redeemed. This man had a deep faith and spirituality the lead him to act with courage.

Value: Social Change

Rosa Parks: Mother Teresa demonstrated her differentiation with her request for exclaustration – a release from her vows to serve the poor of Calcutta, India.

Value: Care for the Poor

These are my heroes. Find some heroes of your own. List them below and the corresponding value:

_____

_____

_____

_____

_____

Be afraid to be your worst enemy
by betraying yourself.

5: COURAGE TO STAY DOWN UNTIL YOU COME UP

*Unrelenting disappointment leaves
you heartsick, but a sudden good
break can turn life around.*
(Proverbs 13:12, MSG)

A lesser-known story of resilience is that of Maxcy Filer, a Compton-based attorney who passed away in 2011. He was a relentless civic leader who advocated for the underprivileged. He sought to serve his civic efforts as an attorney. He started taking the bar exam in 1967 and did not pass until 1991. He took the bar exam forty-eight times before he passed.

What's interesting about his story is that two of his sons, who later also passed the bar exam, were in elementary school when he started taking the exam. Based on the exam costs, he's likely to have paid around $50,000 in fees for the exam. Maybe his main purpose was nothing more than to show people who to stay committed that they can reach their dreams. But how did he do it?

1. Stay hungry.

> *The hungrier you are, the harder*
> *you work.*
> ### *(Proverbs 16:26, CEV).*

The hunger that I'm referring to is not just the one that motivates you to work to feed your family. I'm speaking of the hunger that motivates you to feed your soul. While attempting to pass the text, Mr. Filer fought for equitable representation and led boycotts of banking institutions that refuse to hire black people. He was hungry for justice and that pushed his drive. What are you hungry for?

2. Deepen your purpose. Dig deep.

> *And let us not lose heart and grow*
> *weary and faint in acting nobly and*
> *doing right, for in due time and at*
> *the appointed season we shall reap*
> *if we do not loosen and relax our*
> *courage and faint.*
> ### *(Galatians 6:9, AMPC)*

This teaching says that if you stay down and committed, you will eventually come up. When constructing a building, the higher you go up, the deeper you must go to lay the foundation. It's the same way with your life's purpose. To raise expectations and aim higher, you'll need deeper self-awareness, deeper levels of courage, and deeper levels of focus.

3. Get Up after you fall

Even though good people may be
bothered by trouble seven times,
they are never defeated. (Proverbs
24:16, NCV)

Sometimes you must fight a battle a few times before you win. One of the strategies to defeat a formidable enemy is not to try to take them out but to wear them down. Mr. Filer refused to be worn down. I'm sure there were folks who thought that he should stop trying at year ten, fifteen, and certainly twenty. He was prepared for the long haul because he insisted on getting back up. What he must have known or eventually realized is how close so many people were to success before they gave up.

Be afraid of quitting right before
you succeed.

6: COURAGE TO PIVOT AND START OVER

*When you have faith, you take the
first step even
though you can't see the whole
staircase.*

Ava Duvernay used her gifting to create movies and series, including the recording-breaking, social-shifting documentary When They See Us. After the 2020 racial uprising, several of her films, including Selma and 13th , were nationally recommended as necessary viewing to understand the dynamics of the social issues.

Many people who are in a position that is less than ideal, and who are attempting to make the transition to their ideal place, can learn from her journey.

Duvernay started off doing news reporting. Some of her earlier experiences were not ideal, but they were educational. She moved into publicity because she's a movie nerd. She opened a publicity agency at the age of twenty-seven. She did publicity for almost eighty films and never saw a woman direct. While on film sets, she watched the directors, listened to conversations, and found herself feeling: "I can do this." That was her film school.

Here's the thing—when she made her first three films, she was still doing publicity for studio films. She accepted that she was a director and had her day job. She worked at both jobs until the intended destination could pay her bills. That's how she dealt with the practical risk of moving from publicity to filmmaking.

To manage her internal creative risk, she did the films in secret—because she didn't want the ridicule or questions from clients. It worked! But her success didn't happen all at once. She didn't allow herself to get stuck in what people expected. She followed the unfolding of her new vocational journey.

Two takeaways:
1. 1.It's okay to do things gradually until you're mitigated the practical risks.
2. 2.It's okay to move in obscurity and grow privately until you're strong enough and ready to show the world.

Things to Remember

Generally, there are three stages when one makes a significant life decision – ending, neutral zone, and beginning. Here's a framework to think through the decisions:

Ending

While in the process of change in a particular area of your life, you must recognize when something has come to an end. If you do not embrace the need for change, you will prolong the process of the transition and waste time and energy that could be put to better use. The quicker you let go of the idea that things must stay the same, the sooner you can begin making the transition.

Here are a couple of things to ask yourself and think about in this stage:

1. What is it time to let go of?
2. What activities are you doing that are no longer serving a purpose in your life?
3. What habits and relationships do you need to consider changing or even ending because they no longer serve a purpose in your life?
    a. A key thought is that insanity is doing the same thing over and over and expecting a different result. Naming what must end is powerful in making the transition to a new way of doing things and to a new life.

Example

Going to college means you must let go of the way you thought and acted when you were in high school. In high school, there were probably more people who held you accountable and responsible for your actions.

Now, you must decide to end the irresponsibility and dependency on others because you must grow up and take responsibility for your own actions and their consequences. If you don't make the transition, you will have a hard time figuring things out in college and beyond. So name the things that must end. This should be a constant practice in your life as you evaluate the stage of the change you're in.

1. What actions can you begin to take to help you with the transition?
    a. The longer you wait to delay the change, the harder it will be.
        i. Talking with a coach, therapist, or participating in a support group can be helpful when dealing with the grieving process associated with ending things. In a way, endings are like a death. There is a process of letting go that is not always easy, but it's important that you learn to end well to not leave things unresolved in your mind and heart. See *Choosing a Counselor* at the end of this book.

Neutral Zone

When you begin to move in a new direction, you give yourself the opportunity to make a smoother transition. In between an ending and a beginning something is the neutral zone, also called the desert. This tends to be an uncomfortable time.

There may be times of boredom, restlessness, confusion, fear, panic, self-pity, and distress, but with energy and forethought, it can be a time of reinvention and repositioning for something great.

Sometimes, it feels like you're taking two steps forward and one step backward. Depending on what change is happening in your life, transition can take months, sometimes years and most of the time will be spent in the neutral zone.

I don't say that to discourage you. I say that so you can know what to expect and plan accordingly. Knowing and dealing with the hard truth right away helps you get adjusted more easily than learning it later. Change can only surprise you when you don't expect it.

Expect that your anxiety will rise and motivation will fall. You're not weird or wrong. It is normal that with change and transition, you will feel disoriented and self-doubting. Get comfortable with being uncomfortable. When you stop letting fear and anxiety control your mind, it's like you release yourself from a self-imposed prison. What you are afraid of is rarely as bad as you imagine. Faith in God will sustain you during this time.

Here are a few things to consider during this stage (see ***Bridge the Gaps–Lessons on Self-Awareness, Self-Development, and Self-Care*** (www.thebridge330.com). All chapter references here are to that publication:

1. Holding on to a vision of where you will be is one way to make this time easier. Review the exercise in chapter 8 to remind yourself of this. For the change to stick, you must see the advantage to changing yourself. Think about the kind of person you will be when this is done.

2. Know your values. During this time, anything that you were clear about can become unclear. That's why it's important to know what you assign ultimate importance to in your life so you can build your life the way you want from there.

3. Remember always to be you. Review chapter 2's exercise on the false self. It's tempting to retreat to being what everyone thinks you should be because this discouraging time can make you fall into the pressure of social acceptance which isn't bad unless it moves you away from your calling. Stick to your guns regarding who you are and how you want to be in the world. Over time, you will begin to regain your strength and confidence. Be patient with the process.

4. Think more about what can go right than what can go wrong. Watch yourself-talk. Review chapter 27 – Obstacles from *Bridge the Gaps*. It offers a great tool called STOP. When you change your beliefs, you change your actions.

Much of your success during the transition will depend on what you choose to believe.

5. In this season, there are some things that must be allowed to die and sometimes intentionally brought to death. Old systems of thought, old self-images, and old outlooks need to go for new ones to be brought to life. What are the lessons that you need to learn during this season?

6. Laugh at yourself. Laughter is great medicine and is a valuable tool during these times. Don't take yourself too seriously. You may be all over the place so don't be afraid of your awkwardness in dealing with things. Simply laugh at it.

7. I always recommend a coach, counselor, trusted and wise friend, or a support group to help you during this time. Times when you can be quiet and/or share your feelings in a safe place are helpful to process the emotions around the change in a healthy way. See *Choosing a Counselor* at the end of this book.

Beginning

Now that you have reached the point where the change in your life is complete, and the circumstances around the change are final, there may still be some unresolved emotions that you're having around the change. You got the new house. You changed careers. You started the business. You've been out of prison for a few months and have been employed.

How you thought you would feel might not exactly be how you're feeling, or the beginning of the change may not be as impressive as you thought it would be. In most cases, that is totally normal and to be expected. The true beginning of a change comes when there is a re-alignment internally.

Here are a few things to consider doing or questions to answer to help you finalize a transition (see ***Bridge the Gaps– Lessons on Self-Awareness, Self-Development, and Self- Care*** (www.thebridge330.com). All chapter references here are to that publication:

1. What is the new beginning going to require?
2. What new outlooks, habits, and systems of thoughts do you need to think about and commit to? In the beginning, don't focus on results of what you want to happen. Focus on the process to sustain the change you want.
   a. Remember that maintenance takes just as much work as acquiring, if not more.
3. What mental or emotional obstacles will you need to overcome for this change to be complete? Is it fear? Is it the desire to have the comfort from before? See chapter 27 for ways to deal with adversity.
4. Study people who have gone through the type of change you're going through. Great people don't always show you the confusion and/or hardship they

endured during their transitions. Learning their stories can help you stay encouraged and help you identify yourself with the result of a new beginning. Read their books, listen to their interviews, watch their documentaries, etc. to get a blueprint of the perspective that you need to cultivate and what to expect to make it through the change.

I wish you well with the respective change and transition you're going through now. Use this section to process your thoughts and answer the questions listed above.

Be afraid to stay stuck.

7: THE COURAGE TO STICK TO YOUR GUNS

*Strange how physical courage is
commonplace but moral courage is
rare.*

*The one who lives with integrity
will be helped, but
one who distorts right and wrong
will suddenly fall.*
Proverbs 28:18, HCSB

Legendary actor Denzel Washington tells a story about the movie opportunities he received in his early days of acting. One script was about a black man accused of raping a white woman. They tried to hang the man, but he didn't die. The film was to be a comedy! Considering the gruesome history, this portrayal would have been in poor taste.

Denzel called Sidney Poitier, his mentor and predecessor in the film business. The movie studio had offered him $600,000, and he needed the money. Sidney told him that in the business, the first three or four movies determine how you're perceived. Denzel turned the movie down.

Six months later, he got the offer to make a 1987 Oscar-nominated movie Cry Freedom. The movie is about

the great South African anti-apartheid activist, Steve Biko, who pioneered the black consciousness movement. One of the main points of his ideology was that black people must participate in articulating their own ideals and aspirations. He realized that we have a lot of great black history, but it was also important to craft a great black future rooted in the self-determination of black people. Biko said that if white people determine whether black people are free or enslaved, there is never an opportunity for the black man or woman to choose his or her own destiny.

This was one of Denzel Washington's most important films. Who knows what would have happened if he had acted in that comedy? He refused to compromise and learned to say no, which led him to greatness.

Your soul becomes fortified when you refuse to abandon your principles. The biggest choices you face in life test your integrity. Doing what's right is often inconsistent with convenience, consensus, culture or the clique. That's why you need courage to stick to your guns which will allow others to benefit from your sacrifice.

To break cycles, we must first raise standards. Because of Denzel's life and work, so many artists of this generation stand on his shoulders.

Ten Principles of Effectiveness in Your Calling and Life

In a world that is rapidly changing and full of temptation to compromise one's calling, people need principles, boundaries, and expectations to keep their lives on track. Here's a code of conduct based on proactivity, prevention, and instruction. You'll find more information in my book, ***Bridge the Gaps–Lessons on Self-Awareness, Self-Development, and Self-Care*** (www.thebridge330.com) . All chapter references here are to that publication.

1. Choose your environment and friends wisely.

a. Do not be misled: Bad company corrupts good character. (1 Corinthians 15:33)

b. Read Chapters 22 and 33 of **Bridge the Gaps.**

2. A person's greatness is determined by what it takes to discourage him/her

a. Dear brothers and sisters, is your life full of difficulties and temptations? Then be happy, for when the way is rough, your patience has a chance to grow. So let it grow, and don't try to squirm out of your problems. For when your patience is finally in full bloom, then you will be ready for anything, strong in character, full and complete. (James 1:2-4)

b. Read Chapters 26, 27, 28, and 30 of **Bridge the Gaps**

3. Don't venture past your sphere of knowledge until your sphere of knowledge exceeds your venture.

a. Desire without knowledge is not good — how much more will hasty feet miss the way! (Proverbs 19:2)

b. Read Chapters 7, 9, 16 of **Bridge the Gaps**

4. Work to achieve mastery of yourself and your craft.

a. Do you see someone skilled in their work? They will serve before kings; they will not serve before officials of low rank. (Proverbs 22:29)

b. Read Chapters 2, 3, 4, 5, 6, 10, 13, 14, 21, 24, and 25 of **Bridge the Gaps**

5. Cultivate a vision and work hard to bring it into fruition.

a. All hard work brings a profit, but mere talk leads only to poverty. (Proverbs 14:23)

b. Where there is no vision, the people perish. (Proverbs 29:18)

c. Read Chapters 8, 20 of **Bridge the Gaps**

6. Talk less. Make fewer announcements and more adjustments.
a. Like billowing clouds that bring no rain is the person who talks big but never produces. (Proverbs 25:14)
b. Read Chapters 15 of **Bridge the Gaps**

7. Eliminate distractions and identify your focus.
a. No one serving as a soldier gets entangled in civilian affairs, but rather tries to please his commanding officer. (2 Timothy 2:4)
b. Read Chapters 1, 12, 17, and 29 of ***Bridge the Gaps***

8. You don't have to be great to get started, but you must get started to be great.
a. Do not despise small beginnings. (Zechariah 4:10)
b. Read Chapters 11 of **Bridge the Gaps**

9. Manage your priorities wisely.
a. Teach us to number our days, that we may gain a heart of wisdom. (Psalm 90:12)
b. Read Chapters 18, 19, 23, 43 of **Bridge the Gaps**

10. Learn how to love yourself and others.

a. Let your love abound in knowledge and depth of insight. (Philippians 1:9)

b. Read Chapters 31 to 42 of **Bridge the Gaps**

Be afraid to betray your morals.

8: Courage to Fail

*Sometimes rejection is just
redirection.*

The greatest Los Angeles Laker, Kobe Bryant, retired in the 2016 – 2017 season. Here is a summation of his career - 33,643 points, 18 all-star appearances, 5 NBA championships. His last game was a 60-point performance against the Utah Jazz.

Everyone who has ever played with Kobe has said that his most important quality was his work ethic, but I agree in part. One thing that separated Kobe from everyone else was his tremendous work ethic post-failure. Most people will remember how he ended his career, but I will always remember how he started. I believe that was one of the MOST important moments in his career.

In Kobe Bryant's rookie year, the Los Angeles Lakers made it to the playoffs. The Lakers were playing the Utah Jazz – Game 5, 1997 playoffs. The Jazz led the series 3 -1. The game came down to the wire. The game was tied 89-89. – 10 seconds left in the 4th quarter. Kobe comes down with the ball – drives to the foul line, pulls up and…. AIRBALL. The game goes into overtime. The game continues. Kobe gets the ball on the wing and shoots – AIRBALL. Back-to-Back airballs. 40 seconds left in overtime. Another AIRBALL from Kobe Bryant. With 4 seconds left on the clock, Kobe shoots another AIRBALL.

Can you imagine how he felt after those devastating misses? How would you feel? What would you do?

Here's what Kobe did. That same night, Kobe flew back to LA. He went down to his local high school. The janitor let him in, and he shot the basketball all day. He felt horrible for letting his fans down and knew that folks would dismiss him because of his failure. He came back next season and was determined to vindicate himself. That is exactly what he did.

Bryant's story is a great example of what we should do when we experience failure. The most devastating of losses can make you feel like life is over. Instead of allowing the failure to cause you to breakdown, use it to breakthrough. For Kobe, failure was an opportunity to reinvent himself and his game.

He felt the pain, embarrassment, and loss and used it to fuel the next endeavor. You don't have to be held hostage by the failures of yesterday. Instead, see failure as the price you pay to achieve progress and success. That perspective will lead to perseverance. Perseverance leads to longevity.

To achieve any worthy goal, you will probably face some risk and uncertainty. You don't know what's going to happen. Before you take to risk, decide whether the goal is worth the risk involved. And once you've determined that it is, pull the trigger.

But sometimes, people still don't try to do anything to get closer to their goal because they tend to fall into certain traps. Here is a list of the traps that can keep you from taking the risks you need to take and how you should begin to think about them.

1. "It will be embarrassing" trap – It can feel embarrassing when you fail. Oftentimes because of the possibility of embarrassment, many people believe that failure is to be avoided at all costs. But the only way to be better is to take steps forward, even the small shaky ones. Success comes in taking many small steps and sometimes those steps end up in falls. Don't be ashamed to fail occasionally. The real failure is in not trying. Remember that some of the greatest people endured tremendous failure and embarrassment that they used to fuel their next endeavor.

2. "It's not that important" trap - They second-guess everything they do. People tell themselves that it's not that important. The truth is that if you wait long enough, nothing is important. Unfortunately, the regret will still exist in your mind and heart. You can make amends for the mistakes you make but you can do nothing for the attempts never made.

3. "It's too hard" trap - Some people think everything in life should be easy and when they find out that achievement takes effort, they give up. They are not willing to

focus for a few years, months, and for some people, even a few weeks to reach a goal. They make excuses and walk away.

4.   "It's not fair" trap - Life's not fair, but many people choose not to walk in that reality. These people worry about making life fair than trying to take advantage of the opportunities in front of them. These people are always saying, "I shouldn't have to do this." They compare their journeys to others and their perspective leads to discouragement and ultimately, quitting.

5.   "It's not the right time" trap
It will never be convenient to pursue a goal that worthwhile. You'll have bills, family drama, obligations and deadlines. Don't wait for all the lights to be green before you leave the house. I understand and appreciate all the hardships that come up, but I want you to do something. Just because you can't do it all, start doing something to get closer to your goals. You don't have to do everything. Just do something.

6.   "I don't feel inspired" trap
You don't have to be great to get started, but you must get started to be great. Mediocre people do things when they feel inspired. Great people do things regardless of what their emotions tell them. This doesn't mean they don't take time to process their emotion and pain, but they are not controlled by their emotions.

I hope this list helps to eliminate some of the ways you may have been thinking that have been hurting your progress or keeping you stuck in general. Which traps resonate with you the most? In what ways can you begin to get out of the trap or traps you've identified?

Be afraid to not give your best effort.

9: Courage Tell the Truth about the Past

If we don't face the past, it becomes the present.

In January of 1923, a mob of white people wiped out the black community in Rosewood, Florida after a failed search for a black man accused of raping a white woman. Over several days, the mob destroyed every building and home in that city. Officially, six blacks and two whites were killed, though eyewitness accounts suggest a death toll up to 150. Property was destroyed and fear consumed the survivors as they scattered to other cities in Florida.

The incident faded into history until the survivors, who were children at the time, started speaking up and out in the 1980s. In 1982, St. Petersburg Times journalist Gary Moore resurrected the story until it gained national attention. Civil rights attorney Stephen Hanlon helped the survivors bring a case before the Florida Legislature in 1993.

They won $2.1 million. It was a success! This was the first case where a state paid reparations to black people. It's the only case—but it doesn't have to be the last one. Fact-finding forums for any occasions can be done, not just for the financial compensation but also for the moral, spiritual, and emotional closure of the acknowledgment. Such cases are a major part of the country's needed healing.

John Singleton made the movie Rosewood when he was twenty-six years old. Rosewood is a movie about a 1923 racist lynch mob attack in (corrected) an African American community in Rosewood, Florida. Singleton wanted to ensure that black people had the ability to tell their own stories.

He wanted to ensure that the falsehoods of black people being benign during their persecution was eradicated. His intention was to uncover the untold history of black people fighting back against their oppression in the South. Few movies have been made about black American's experience with white terrorism, partly because it goes against Hollywood's function to create movies wrapped in heroism. Singleton was pressured by Hollywood executives to change his movie's messaging, but he refused.

He didn't work for four years after its release. Rosewood was not commercially successful, but his movie now sits in the Library of Congress. Its release sparked tremendous dialogue about the race riots in the 20th century. Instead of trying to make more money, Singleton chose to do something important. He brought to light the undercurrent of a progressive and healing paradigm for black America.

The mainstream American narrative that I was taught tells us that great strides were made through these pieces of legislation, and that America now provides equal opportunities for black people to participate in the social, political, and economic order without interruption.

The problem is that, when you take time to review America's complicated and imperfect history—specifically the history of black Americans—you will quickly notice how the dominant culture's perspective either subtly acknowledges or very conveniently passes over the ugly truths and injustices of America's racist past, including:

- Between 1877 and 1950: **Jim Crow** along with convict leasing and more than 4,000 lynchings of black Americans.
- The 1930s through 1960s: **Predatory housing practices** against black Americans when they were kept out of the legitimate home-mortgage market between.
- The 1950s: **Blatant refusal to desegregate schools**, despite legislation. Fourteen Mississippi school districts refused for fifteen years to desegregate schools, even after the 1954 Brown v. Board of Education decision.

This is a history that black people did not choose, but it's not a history that is obscure or unavailable. These facts are often deliberately left out of the general discourse because the victors often have an *a la carte* relationship with the past. The victors, not the victims, write history, often in their own favor and with an exponential reflection on what favors them or disfavors those oppressed, without acknowledging root causes.

As the victims rise to positions of power, the narrative that was once told is re-evaluated. Because of the evolving landscape of America's racial make-up, the once-vague understandings of racial injustice become clear and subsequently indict a nation that purports to represent liberty and justice for all. As Frederick Douglas alluded, the story of the master doesn't need more narrators. The story of the slave does.

What can we do about this today? Let's tell the *real story* to create a better future.

> *Be afraid to let the past become the present.*

Choosing a Counselor[i]

In choosing a counselor, always keep in mind that you are a consumer. You are purchasing a service from a professional and have choices about whether you want to begin such a relationship. These are some questions you might ask:

1) What are your techniques of training, experience, and specialization?

2) Are there particular techniques you use?

3) Will you discuss my treatment plan with me?

4) What happens if we disagree about my goals?

5) Are you licensed by or registered with the state?

6) Have you ever had a charge of unethical conduct brought against you?

7) For what length of time do you usually treat clients?

8) Is there anyone with whom you will be discussing my case?

9) Have you had experience with other people in similar situations?

10) Do you charge for an initial consultation?

11) Do you charge for a telephone consultation?

12) How much do you charge for each counseling session?

13) Will my insurance pay for this counseling?

14) How long will our appointments be?

15) If I decide that I would like to work with you, are there any other interviews that you require me to complete?

Many therapists gain clients through word of mouth, and certainly hearing good things about a therapist is a promising sign that the therapist that was good for your friend might also be good for you. But just as you won't necessarily like all your friend's friends, you won't necessarily "click" with your friend's choice of therapist.

You need to like and respect your therapist, or you will not be open to what they say to you. You should also feel comfortable enough with your therapist that you could say anything to them and you would not feel that they would judge you or think less of you. This is very important, since there may be things that you tell a therapist that you will never tell another person. So it is very important to feel that you trust them and you trust their judgment.

After deciding on a therapist, it is a good idea to give a therapist at least two sessions before you make up your mind about whether you can work with them. If you still feel uncomfortable, it might be time to find another one. You should also be prepared to feel nervous and uncomfortable at times with your therapist. After all, they are not meant to be a friend who will nod and agree with everything you say. Sometimes therapists can make you feel very uncomfortable indeed, as they slowly move you toward areas in your life that are blocking you that you haven't wanted to deal with. This is where it is important that you have that initial liking and trusting relationship. When things start to get hard in therapy, you need to feel reassured that your therapist is there trying to make your life better and is ultimately on your side.

Occasionally, you will get angry with your therapist, and a good therapist will be able to cope with that and not get angry back at you. An angry therapist is not a good sign, and although rare lapses are acceptable, since we are all human, a therapist who routinely displays frustration at your slow progress or inability to move past a certain difficulty in your life, is not the right therapist for you.

The best relationship is where you can look back and see that during the difficult times in your life journey, your therapist was there, like a patient parent, listening, hoping for, and observing your recovery. When you finally get to a resolution, they are almost as pleased as you are!

Resources

If you, or someone you know, is in crisis, please seek help immediately. Contact the following organizations for information about twenty-four-hour crisis services in your area:

The National Suicide Prevention Lifeline's twenty-four-hour, toll-free crisis hotline, 1.800.273.TALK (1.800.273.8255) can put you into contact with your local crisis center, which can tell you where to seek immediate help in your area.

The SAMHSA Substance Abuse Treatment Facility Locator and the SAMHSA 24/7 Treatment and Referral line at 1.800.662.4357 provide referrals to alcohol, substance abuse, and dual-diagnosis treatment facilities, including facilities that offer sliding scale fees and other special payment arrangements. Dual diagnosis services provide integrated treatment for individuals who have both an alcohol or substance abuse problem and a mental illness. They will help you find the facilities that most closely match your needs.

The Child-Help USA 1.800.4.A.CHILD (1.800.422.4453) crisis line assists both child and adult survivors of abuse, including sexual abuse. The hotline, staffed by mental health professionals, also provides treatment referrals.

To locate therapists, you can go to this link http://www.mentalhealthamerica.net/finding-therapy or www.mentalhealth.gov for referrals.

Do everything you can to seek help. Please don't hesitate to contact a trained and licensed counselor for assistance. Whatever you're going through, you don't have to do it alone.

What Is TheBridge330?

TheBridge330 mentoring program was started to provide individuals with the tools to be self-reflective, productive in their purpose, and attentive to their well-being. The values that undergird the program and its mission focus on social change, restoring hope in vulnerable communities, and paving a pathway to emotional health. The name TheBridge330 was chosen for two reasons:

1) TheBridge - As I served in my community over a period of years, there were grassroot realities that consistently emerged, issues like incarceration, recidivism, illiteracy, the long-term effects of child abuse, and fatherlessness. For a bridge to be built for passage over obstacles, the two primary obstacles that need to be addressed are hatred and ignorance, within and without the community. The program is designed to raise awareness of these issues and bring resources to bear.

2) John 3:30 (CEV) says, "Jesus must become more important, while I become less important."
I learned this passage from the Bible in church as a teenager. In essence, it talks about living like

Jesus. As I studied his teachings, several of them emerged as cornerstone philosophies for real healing and social change:

-Take care of the "least of these" (the hungry, thirsty, the stranger, the naked, sick, the imprisoned). (Matthew 25)
-Be like the Good Samaritan who cares for the vulnerable and abandoned. (Luke 10)
-Defend those attacked by unjust and merciless accusers. Then provide the guidance and counsel to help the accused live a life of purpose and turn from the sinful path. (John 8)
-Meet the needs of those without guidance—the sheep without a shepherd. (Mark 6:34)
-Overturn the tables; disrupt the practices of the unscrupulous businesspeople who extort the poor. (John 2:15)

I realized that the example of Jesus is what can truly change our world. That was contrary to what I was living and seeing around me. So I chose to live it out. I've had some tough days and made my fair share of mistakes. At the same time, I was privileged to have the safety and resources needed to find my way to my purpose. Jesus says, "To whom much is given, from him much will be required" (Luke 12:48, NKJV). I chose to teach through writing. To find out more about my mission, check out the following books:

Bridge the Gaps – Lessons on Self-Awareness, Self-Development and Self-Care (Reference: BTG)
-A life coaching framework that provides tools to cultivate a heightened sense of identity and purpose, a growth mindset, and a greater level of emotional health.

The Bridge to Change – Mentoring Tools for Parents, Teachers, Coaches, and Counselors (Reference: TBTC)
-A mentoring guide that provides tools for ending unproductive beliefs, behaviors, and attitudes, while healing the multigenerational transmission of trauma, and leveraging the resilience of people to build a healthier culture.

You can find these books at https://www.barnesandnoble.com, https://www.amazon.com or www.thebridg330.store.

About the Author

Jonathan Frejuste is the creator of TheBridege330, a program whose mission is to provide quality mentoring tools and resources to underserved, under-resourced, and vulnerable communities in ways that support sustained social change, a restoration of hope, and an avenue to emotional health. He is also an Associate Coach with The Center for Emotional Development. He is certified in the emotional measures EQi and EQ 360. He has coached leaders ranging from directors of law enforcement agencies to senior spiritual leaders. He worked as an auditor with Deloitte and Touche, where he earned his CPA (certified public accountant) license and serves as a senior financial planner with Ernst and Young, where he earned his Series 65 Registered Investment Advisor License. He served as a life skills coach at the Somerset Home for Temporarily Displaced Children and was certified as a behavioral assistant with the state of New Jersey's Children's System of Care. He serves schools and non-profits as a speaker, workshop facilitator, and a coach, using the skills he's acquired through his diverse background to provide people with tools and resources to promote and support individual and community well-being.

IG: @tb330life
Website: www.thebridge330.com
E-mail: jon@thebridge330.com

End Notes

[i] Mchugh, Beth "Finding a Good Therapist", *Your Online Counselor,* 2007
http://youronlinecounselor.com/Articles/finding-good-therapist.htm

www.ingramcontent.com/pod-product-compliance
Lightning Source LLC
Chambersburg PA
CBHW060529030426
42337CB00021B/4196